CHILD CUSTODY & VISITATION IN CALIFORNIA

PREPARING FOR THE BATTLE AHEAD & STRATEGIES FOR WINNING THE WAR

SHAUNA M. ALBRIGHT, Esq.
CHILD CUSTODY & DIVORCE ATTORNEY

Printed in the United States of America.

ISBN: 978-1-63385-346-1

LEGAL DISCLAIMER

This book is designed to provide information about the subject matter covered. It is provided with the understanding that the author and the publisher are not engaged in rendering legal, accounting, and other professional services. This book does not constitute an attorney-client relationship in California, another state, or territory. If legal advice or other professional assistance is required, the services of a competent professional should be sought.

Every effort has been made to make this book as complete and accurate as possible. This book should be used only as a general guide, and not as the ultimate source of the subject matter covered.

The author and the publisher shall have neither liability nor responsibility to any person or entity with respect to any loss or damage caused or alleged to be caused directly or indirectly by the information covered in this book.

I dedicate this book lovingly to my mother, Jacqueline, for teaching me at an early age to believe in myself, to walk in faith, to love others, and to have a purpose in life. I know you are smiling from above as you continue to be the light that shines brightly upon me.

CONTENTS

INTRODUCTION

We all wish that life was easy. Unfortunately, it's not always so simple. This doesn't mean you're faulty or that anything is wrong with you. It just means that life did what life does best.

It took its course.

If you've purchased this book, you're most likely facing a life and family-changing situation. You're trying to decide custody and visitation arrangements for your precious child or children. Frankly, this is one of the toughest things you will do in your entire life. There are no words strong enough to express how difficult it will be.

In this situation, it's easy to let feelings of sadness, guilt, anger, and fear fill your head—not to mention the endless sea of "what ifs." "What if I had done something differently?" "What if I had been home more?" "What if I can't do this on my own?"

PLEASE STOP.

While it's human nature to second guess ourselves, giving into these doubts will only make matters worse and won't solve the problem at hand. That's why I'm going to ask something of you:

I want you to put all negative thoughts and judgments aside.

You are not damaged or faulty. You are not a bad parent. You are not a bad person. You are simply human.

In any custody situation, I highly encourage parents to co-parent. **Co-parenting** is when two parents unite to raise their child even after they divorce, separate, or are no longer living together. When parents separate or divorce, it can be traumatizing for the child. The idea behind co-parenting is that both parents collaborate in an amicable way when making decisions about their child.

Though ideal, co-parenting can be difficult.

Each parent has a unique view of the situation at hand, often without taking into consideration what is in the best interest of the child. Raising a child when each parent has a different view of how to raise that child can be emotionally taxing on everyone—especially the child.

Sometimes, the other parent may be unreasonable. The other parent may want to battle for the sake of battling—simply because he is angry or hurt at the way things ended. He wants to win, regardless of what is in the best interest of his child. Other times, a parent may be upset because the other parent has moved on emotionally. She may want to make it difficult for the other parent to have a relationship with his child. However, one thing remains constant: the child is stuck in the middle of all this.

When this happens, you feel trapped. Giving in to unreasonable requests of the other parent isn't in the best interest of your child. So, what can you do? You can prepare.

To prepare for a custody battle in a situation where the other parent is highly unreasonable isn't an act of selfishness. It's an act of responsibility and protection. At the end of the day, you want to do what's best for your child.

Doing what's best for your child is what this book is all about. My purpose in writing this book is simple: I want to give you the tools you need to represent both yourself and the best interest of your child in the state of California.

I know this is easier said than done. There are thousands of scenarios you could be facing at this very instant. Maybe you can't come to an agreement on visitation. Maybe both of you want your child to live with you primarily. You might even be facing a situation in which you feel your child would be in danger if left alone with the other parent.

These are terrifying situations.

Unless you and the other parent agree on a parenting agreement, at some point, the judge will make final child custody orders. The judge will decide where your child will live primarily, what the holiday visitation schedule will be, what the regular visitation schedule will entail, and other issues related to child custody and visitation.

This book will help you plan for the process you're now facing. My goal is to give you confidence by providing a wealth of information that I have acquired over the years. I am hopeful that this information will give you a better overall understanding of the child custody and visitation process.

In this book, I will cover the following:

- How to put your best case forward
- What to look for when choosing an attorney
- What a Request for Order and a Responsive Declaration entail
- Tips on what the judge is looking for
- How to create compelling evidence that is relevant to your case
- What mediation means
- How to argue your case in front of the judge
- Factors the judge may consider
- What to do if the judge doesn't agree with your request

It's important to remember that these are just tips. Every situation is different. This book is valuable, but in the world of family law, there is no exact science. Dealing with the court system is an art, not a science.

In family law, there's no one size fits all. Your facts are going to be different from another person's facts. Also, your story will differ from another family's story. No two outcomes will be the same because no two families are the same.

My goal is for you to use this book as a guide to navigating the laws of California as they relate to child custody and visitation. This book is your unofficial roadmap to success. I'm not a judge, but I am an attorney. Through the years, I've helped people just like you deal with child custody and visitation issues.

In closing this introduction, I want you to think about something: People can and do overcome these situations. They build new, happy, and healthy lives. They can start over and become stronger and better parents than they ever imagined they could be.

Always remember that you will rise above this. It just takes time and patience. You are not alone. You will find support, strength, and hope when you least expect it.

Are you ready to get started?

CHAPTER 1

CHILD CUSTODY ACTION

It's no secret that child custody disagreements can bring about a lot of anger and hostility. After all, no one wants to be limited to seeing her child on certain days and weekends. Unfortunately, this is a reality of separation and divorce.

What It Means and How to Start

In beginning any child custody battle, there is an underlying concept to remember: Judges have to consider what is in the best interest of your child.

That's why planning your strategy isn't just important—it's crucial. Your strategy can make or break what happens in the long run as you work out the exact specifications of your child custody and visitation plan.

The good news is that understanding the ins and outs of this concept is what this book is all about. In this book, you're going to learn to think like an attorney—no matter how the system hits you. If you have time to plan, you'll know how to do it. If the other parent serves you with custody papers when you least expect it, you'll know what to do.

In this chapter, you're going to learn how the legal system in California works. This knowledge is important, so don't skip ahead. Even if you know the process already, you may gain new tips and ideas.

Please know that this chapter is a bit technical, so you may want to take notes. You can also access local county court websites as a resource. On these websites, you will find the forms and the local rules for the county where the judge will hear your case.

Navigating Your Options

There are two common ways to start a child custody action in the state of California.

The first option is to file a **Petition to Establish Parental Relationship,** which opens the door for a Request for Order. (The RFO will be explained on page 22.) The petitioner files the Petition to Establish Parental Relationship in the county where the child resides.

The second option is to file a **Petition for Dissolution**, which says you plan to seek a divorce or legal separation. The petitioner files the Petition for Dissolution in the county where the petitioner has resided for the past three months.

Both of these options open the door to addressing custody and visitation matters.

As a side note, a parent can open a child support case through the Department of Child Support Services (DCSS). If you receive a document from the Department of Child Support Services, please respond in a timely manner. Failure to respond can result in orders that you may not be in agreement with, such as a child support order based on inaccurate income information, you being deemed the father (if you are challenging paternity), you being required to provide health insurance, and a host of other potential orders. I suggest that you seek the advice of a knowledgeable professional right away should you receive documents from DCSS.

A Petition to Establish Parental Relationship is the vehicle for unmarried parents. This document means that you're legally establishing who the father of a child is. Either parent may file a Petition to Establish Parental Relationship. In understanding this concept, it's important to know that the state can order child support once the parents have established paternity.

This process may involve a DNA test to prove who the father of a child is. A judge would order these tests if one party objects to paternity. That said, the objecting party usually pays for the DNA tests. If there is no objection, the state will determine that the father listed on the petition is the father of the child.

Regardless of which petition you use, the petition, along with a blank response (for the other person to fill out) and other accompanying documents must be **served** on the other person. The official term for this action is **Service of Process**, and it gives the other person notice of what's going on. Service of Process is one of the most critical steps in getting the case to move forward. Until the serving of the petition occurs, the court generally does not have power over the other person and cannot make any orders.

So, how do you serve someone?

The most common way to serve a person a petition is by personal service. Personal Service simply means that the documents are handed to the person. You can hire an agency or enlist the help of a friend who is 18 years of age or older, of sound mind, and not a party to the action to serve the petition for you. It's important to note that YOU cannot be the server.

Once you serve the other person, there is a general time frame of 30 days for the other person to file and serve a Response to the Petition to Establish Parental Relationship or the Petition for Dissolution. The response can be served by mail. Similar to serving a petition, the person responding to a petition cannot directly serve the response.

If the other person fails to respond within the required time frame, the moving party (the person who filed the petition) can request an entry of default and file a default judgment with the court. The judgment allows the person who filed the petition to ask the judge to make orders regarding paternity, custody/visitation, child support and other orders without the consent of the other person.

I highly urge anyone who is served with a petition to take it seriously. Failure to respond promptly may result in you being declared the father even if you are not the biological father. Because of this, you may be ordered to pay child support for a child that is not biologically related to you.

After the other person is served with the petition, the person who served the petition must also fill out a **Proof of Service** and file it with the court. A Proof of Service lets the court know that the other person has been served. Without a Proof of Service filed with the court, there is a strong possibility that the case will not be able to move forward until the court receives it. The person who served the response must also fill out and file a Proof of Service.

If you cannot locate the other person and can demonstrate to the judge that you have made every reasonable effort to do so, you can request the court's permission to serve the other person through publication. This method allows you to publish a notice in a newspaper located in the county of the other person's last known address.

Assuming that service was completed correctly, the judge will make a ruling on the issue of paternity at a future hearing.

Because service of process is a critical step in getting your case moving along, I highly suggest you consult with an experienced attorney or an organization that may offer free legal advice. Some courts provide free assistance to people representing themselves.

PETITIONER AND RESPONDENT—WHICH ARE YOU?

When you're dealing with initial court actions, you will see two words a lot: **petitioner** and **respondent**. It's critical to know the difference.

The **petitioner is the person who files the petition**—whether it is a Petition to Establish Dissolution or a Petition to Establish Parental Relationship. If you are the person who filed the petition, you are the petitioner in every document that you file after that for that specific case. The **respondent is the person who files the response**—whether it is a Response to a Petition for Dissolution or a Response to a Petition to Establish Parental Relationship. Once the petition is filed, a case number will be assigned to that case. All future documents related to that case will be filed under that case number.

Please know that it does not matter if you are the petitioner or the respondent. I want to assure you that I have never witnessed a judge making orders for or against a person based on whether that person is the petitioner or the respondent.

The Definition of Request for Order (RFO)

Assuming there is a finding that the other person is the father of your child, you now have the right to ask for temporary orders regarding the life and financial support of your child during the divorce or separation process. This action is called a **Request for Order** (abbreviated as **RFO**).

The other parent (who, for the sake of example, will be Dad) has the same rights as well. Either parent can file an RFO requesting custody and visitation orders.

An RFO requesting custody and visitation means you're asking the judge to establish a temporary parenting plan for your child until a final parenting plan can be determined. It is a document that you can fill out that gives you a way of asking the judge to get involved. It gives the judge an idea of exactly what you would like to have happen when it comes to the custody and care of your child.

In an RFO, you will have the opportunity to prepare a written statement outlining your proposed parenting plan and why you believe your proposed parenting plan is in the best interest of your child. In addition, you will have an opportunity to attach your evidence and third-party witness statements.

An RFO is a separate document from the Petition for Dissolution or the Petition to Establish Parental Relationship. The ability to file an RFO comes by way of filing one of these petitions. Therefore, you'll file one of these petitions either before or at the same time you file an RFO.

At some point after filing the RFO requesting temporary custody and visitation orders, you will be given a hearing date, which is when you will appear before the judge. On this date, you will have the opportunity to tell the judge what you are asking for and why.

Once you file your RFO requesting custody and visitation orders with the court, you will need to serve the other party with a conformed copy of the RFO and a blank Responsive Declaration(a form for the other parent to fill out). The conformed copy will be stamped by the court and will have the hearing date as well as any other relevant information related to the hearing.

The general time frame to serve the other parent with the court conformed copy of the RFO is 16 court days before the hearing date plus five extra calendar days if service is by mail. As mentioned previously, YOU cannot be the one to serve the other parent. For more information on service, please review California Code of Civil Procedure section 1005(b).

The Definition of a Responsive Declaration to Request for Order

When a parent is served with an RFO and other documents filed with the court, that parent will need to file and serve on the other parent a **Definition of a Responsive Declaration to Request for Order** (also known as a **Responsive Declaration**). A Responsive Declaration is the responding parent's opportunity to tell his side of the story.

In this document, the responding parent will have the opportunity to address the allegations and issues the

RFO raised. The responding parent can also bring up issues related to custody and visitation regarding the other parent. The responding parent can share with the judge the custody and visitation plan he believes is in the best interest of his child and why. Please note that the "why" part of this document is crucial.

Taking the time to actually comply with this procedure is vital. If a parent does not file a Responsive Declaration, there could be some consequences.

First, it could result in the judge making custody and visitation orders that the non-responding parent may not agree with. Second, the judge could order the non-responding parent to pay attorney's fees should the case need to be continued to give the parent and opportunity to file a Responsive Declaration.

Additionally, not filing a response may make it look as though the non-responding parent does not oppose the other parent's RFO. Think of it like this: if the other parent wants the child to live with her during the week and you don't say no in the form of a response, your lack of response may appear to mean, "Yes I agree." That's not a good thing if you believe it would be in the best interest of your child to live with you during the week.

In practical terms, the judge will probably give a parent at least one pass if he doesn't file a Responsive Declaration. The judge will want to hear from both parents in order to make decisions that reflect the best interest of the child. Therefore, if this lack of response is an isolated incident, the judge may continue the matter to give the non-responding parent an opportunity to respond and a chance to prepare.

However, this is not guaranteed. For this reason, it is always best to file a Responsive Declaration to avoid any possible chance of the judge making orders without you having the opportunity to respond.

What happens if you fail to file a Responsive Declaration, and the judge decides to continue the matter?

If a judge does continue the matter, he can make interim orders. These are temporary orders encompassing issues such as your visitation schedule and where your child will live primarily. You may not like these orders, but interim orders are enforceable until a judge modifies the orders at the next hearing. Also, the parties can agree to a different parenting plan. The agreement should be in writing and submitted to the Court to avoid any confusion. Generally speaking, a judge is happy when the parties can come to an agreement. Therefore, filing a timely response serves you best.

As a practical tip, the person requesting custody and visitation orders can also request other orders at the same time, including child support, spousal support (alimony), and attorney fees from the other parent. The requesting party can request these orders on the same RFO. If requesting money orders, the requesting party must fill out an Income and Expense Declaration (I&E). The I&E is a form that asks about each party's income and obligations. It must be filed with the RFO and served on the other party along with a blank I&E for the other party to fill out and file with the court.

The Real Reason You Need an RFO

A Request for Order serves an essential purpose: It gives you the ability to ask the judge to issue temporary orders while your case is pending resolution. When parents separate, there tends to be a lot of uncertainty. Where will the child live? What school will the child attend? An RFO is simply a way of asking the judge to make orders until he has determined what the permanent orders should be.

You can use an RFO for many things. For starters, you can use an RFO to ask for specific custody and visitation arrangements. For example, you may request that your child primarily lives with you instead of the other parent during the divorce or separation process. If you're not seeking primary custody, you can use an RFO to establish a visitation plan. Filing an RFO is helpful in addressing the issue of one parent not allowing the other parent to see the child.

You can use an RFO to ask for supervised visitation if you feel that your child is in danger. Please note that you can also request a "No Visitation Order" to protect your child. We will cover further details on these concepts in the next section.

The Importance of Emergency Hearings

It's important to know that the court handles emergencies differently than regular RFOs. Do not forget that. Your situation may require a judge to act quickly to protect your child, and you have the right to ask a judge to hear your case immediately in the state of California.

There are some reasons you would take action in this respect, including concerns of child abuse, the other parent using illegal drugs, or the possibility of the other parent taking the child out of the state or country without permission. These emergency situations warrant immediate action.

In such cases, you would need to file for an **Emergency Hearing**. In legal terms, we refer to this as an **Ex-Parte Hearing**. Consider it your panic button in the legal system. You would request this if you believe the child is not safe with the other parent.

Emergency hearings take place the same day you file or one business day later depending on the county you live in. In taking this action, you're essentially telling the judge: "This can't wait. I need to be heard immediately."

When asking the judge to make emergency orders, you can also request for the other parent to have supervised visitations or no visitations at all. Supervised visitations are when a third party supervises visitations to ensure the child's safety. In the case of supervised visitations, you can request that a friend or family member supervise the visitations, or you can request a professional monitor to supervise the visits. Just know that a professional monitor can be costly. That said, judges will order the parent needing supervised visitations to pay for the supervision unless there is an income disparity. Supervised visitations usually occur during the day on specified days and only for a few hours.

If it is needed, it's crucial that you file for an emergency hearing without delay to protect your child. Too much can change too fast. The longer you wait to address issues related to your child's safety, the more you run the risk of losing credibility with the judge.

For example, if the other parent took your child out of the state without your knowledge and you waited several months to request that the other parent return your child, the judge may determine that you waited too long and may not address your concerns at an emergency hearing.

It's important to note that not all situations qualify for an emergency hearing. While a situation may seem urgent to a parent, a judge may not deem it as such. It is important to make sure an emergency hearing request is valid and not a waste of the judge's time.

Primary Physical Custody v. Joint Physical Custody

In almost every custody battle, the argument of who the child will live with primarily is at the heart of the battle. In most of my cases, this is what the parents are fighting over: physical custody. Physical custody determines the physical living arrangements for your child. The parent who has the child the majority of the time is referred to as the primary custodial parent and thus has **primary physical custody** of the child. Generally speaking, where your child lives primarily will determine what school district your child attends. This rule is not set in stone, but judges follow this trend.

There are times when a judge can order that parents share **joint physical custody**, meaning that both parents will have frequent and continuous contact with the child. In other words, the child will live with each parent for significant periods of time. Joint physical custody does not necessarily mean that the child will live equally with each parent.

50/50 custody is an informal term you will hear often in family court. 50/50 means that the parents share the child equally. An example of a 50/50 custodial arrangement is when the child lives with one parent one week and the other parent the next week.

Joint Legal Custody v. Sole Legal Custody

When there is a custody battle, the question of which parent will make the legal decisions for their child is often front and center. Legal custody determines which parent will make decisions about the child such as what school the child will attend, medical decisions concerning the child, and more. Unless there is a good reason not to, courts generally will order **joint legal custody** in which both parents communicate with each other to jointly make non-emergency decisions for their child.

If the other parent is not fit to make legal decisions about your child, you can ask a judge to make an order that you have **sole legal custody**. There are times when it is clearly not in the best interest of the child for parents to share joint legal custody; such as, when one parent is abusive or when one parent refuses to address their child's medical condition. For example, let's say that your child has a condition that requires medical decisions on a regular basis, yet the other parent continues to put up roadblocks so that your child cannot get the care he needs. In this situation, there may be good cause for requesting sole legal custody of your child. Another example of when you may want to request sole legal custody of your child is when the other parent has been an absentee parent for a significant period of time. In the end, it will be up to you as the parent to make the request for sole legal custody and provide the reasons for the request.

As a practical tip, I have found that judges frown upon a parent who insists on having sole legal custody without valid reasons. Some judges may see this as an unwillingness of that parent to co-parent with the other parent. Be very careful when asking for sole legal custody, and make sure you have valid reasons as to why the other parent should not share in the legal decision-making.

Temporary Custody Orders v. Final Custody Orders—What's the Difference?

At first glance, you may think that the difference is evident. Temporary custody and visitation orders are short-term while final custody and visitation orders are long-term. This way of thinking is correct in practical terms but does not play out this way most of the time in court.

Generally speaking, the first hearing on custody and visitation will be to establish temporary child custody and visitation orders. These temporary orders can be modified several times as needed before the final orders are actually made.

At some point, the judge will set the case for a trial to determine final orders (unless you and the other parent agree on a parenting plan). The hard truth is that judges rarely make final custody and visitation orders that are staunchly different from temporary custody orders because judges are hesitant to change a parenting plan that is in place and is working. While changes might be rare, they can happen. It just means that it will be an uphill battle to convince the judge to make the changes if that parenting plan is working for the children.

Why is this important? It is important because temporary orders that are made early on in your case, either by a court order or by an agreement between the parents, will have an impact on the final orders. If you do not believe a temporary parenting plan is in the best interest of your child, you may want to think twice about agreeing to it. It may become status quo, which could make it difficult for you to convince a judge to deviate grossly from the orders later on.

You can always request a modification of temporary and final custody orders. The judge may modify the orders if he believes there is good cause to do so. What constitutes a good reason to request a modification of current orders is subjective. You will need to file a new RFO and show why the current orders need modification.

A judge will want to know why you believe it is in the best interest of your child to modify the current orders. Perhaps your work schedule has changed. Maybe you lived in another county and now have moved closer to your child. It could be that your child is failing in school while living with the other parent primarily. These are only a few examples to consider when requesting a modification to a custody and visitation order.

CHAPTER 2

BUILDING YOUR WINNING STRATEGY BEFORE THE BATTLE BEGINS

One of the most common mistakes people make in the process of a child custody action is not planning enough. The building of your case should start before you even go into battle. It's your preparation phase.

Think of it like this: if you're going to fight a war, you don't just start fighting. You first train and prepare. The same goes for a child custody case. Before you begin, you plan your strategy. This is the benefit of filing an RFO. If you're the filer, you have time to line up your army of evidence because you're the initiator.

The Responsive Declaration, however, is a little different. If there's a surprise attack, you might not have a lot of time to prepare as you only have a certain amount of time to respond.

For example, if you're served, you have to respond nine court days before the hearing, plus five extra calendar days for mailing, which can be challenging. That said, if you are the respondent, you should line up your ducks in the same way you would if you filed the RFO. You still need to prepare evidence and strategize for the battle.

(Please note that there may be different mailing time frame requirements if you live out of the country or out of the state.)

What to Include in an RFO or a Responsive Declaration

In either an RFO or a Responsive Declaration, you want to include in your declaration the facts that are relevant to the issue of custody and visitation. The judge wants to know what your proposed parenting plan is and why you believe your proposed parenting plan is in the best interest of your child.

For example, if you are requesting that your child live with you during the week and visit with the other parent every other weekend, you will need to explain why this plan is in the best interest of your child. Remember to be specific about what time the visitations will start and end.

Other important considerations include where the visitation exchanges will occur. If the other parent is hostile, you may want to propose drop off and pick up in a well-lit, public area.You may also want to include in your declaration your desire for dividing special days such as Mother's Day, Father's Day, your child's birthday, your birthday, summer visitations, and any other holidays.

If you plan to take summer vacations, you will want to include this in your declaration as well. If you believe the other parent would benefit from a parenting class or that both of you would benefit from a co-parenting class, you will want to include this recommendation in your declaration.

As outlined in the following section, there are factors the judge will consider in determining what parenting plan is in the best interest of your child. As a rule of thumb, you should include any other factors that you believe are important for the judge to consider. Further, please note that you should attach your declaration and other evidence you would like the judge to consider to your RFO. Third-party witness statements can be filed separately or as an additional attachment.

Factors the Judge May Consider

The judge will consider many factors. In this section, I'll summarize some of these factors, but keep in mind that this list is not exhaustive. As previously stated, no two families are the same. I encourage you to include any and all facts that are relevant to your case in your RFO or your Responsive Declaration. Please take them into consideration as you plan your personal strategy.

1. **Safety of the Child** - The judge will take it into consideration if one parent has committed child abuse or abuse against the other parent. The judge will also consider the habitual use of illegal drugs or prescribed medications as well as consistent alcohol abuse. The court will take into consideration either parent's criminal history. In addition, the judge will take into consideration the criminal history and other issues of concern as it relates to a parent's significant other, especially when this person is around the child.

2. **Child's Preference** - If the child is 14 years or older, the judge will give the child's preference heavy consideration. Even if the child is under the age of 14, the judge may consider the child's wishes depending on the circumstances. Children have feelings too, and judges ultimately want to ensure their emotional and physical safety. If a child has a strong reason why he would like to live with one parent, a judge will most likely listen. A judge, however, does not have to agree with the child.

3. **Work Hours** - If you are a mom who works graveyard shifts while the dad works 8 a.m. to 4 p.m., it may be an uphill battle to argue that the children should live with you primarily during the week. The judge will want to know who would be taking care of the children when you are working at night. With that said, the judge will consider other factors too. As a practical tip, you may

want to consider changing your work schedule if you believe your schedule may hurt your case.

4. **Emotional Bonds and Relationships with Each Parent** If Mom has been the primary caregiver and Dad has been traveling for work most of the child's life, the judge will consider this in making a determination of where the child should primarily live. On that same note, if one parent has been an absentee parent for most of the child's life, it will be an uphill battle for the absentee parent to ask for the child to live with him primarily.

5. **Cooperation** - The judge will consider which parent is more likely to encourage a child to have a relationship with the other parent. It is imperative to remember this. While you don't have to give in to unreasonable requests made by the other parent, you also don't want to appear petty in front of the judge.

6. **The Child's Routine** - Has a precedent (what the child is used to) been set? A judge will be reluctant to upset a child's pattern that has been in place for a lengthy amount of time. For example, if you and the other parent agreed to an informal visitation schedule outside of court and this pattern is working well for the child, the judge will be reluctant to change that pattern. If you do not feel an arrangement is in the best interest of your child, you may want to think twice before you agree to it informally. It could be difficult to convince the judge to modify that informal agreement later down the road.

7. **Therapy** - If your child is in therapy, the judge will want to know why and who is responsible for taking the child to therapy. If one parent is not active in therapy or is against it, this may raise a concern for the judge

as to that parent's ability to provide an emotionally safe environment for the child. Also, you may want to request that your child start therapy if he is not handling the separation well. If the other parent is against it without a good reason, you should point that out to the judge.

Planning an Evidence-Based Strategy

To strategize as either a petitioner or respondent, you need to know how courts operate. Courts work in a defined manner. They're evidence-based systems. In other words, showing up to court and hoping the judge will hear your story isn't enough.

We've all known someone who doesn't stand by their word. The same is true for the judge. In family court, people often don't tell the truth. Everyone has a story, but some of those stories may be fabricated. Judges know this. Because of this, facts that support stories hold more weight than words alone. After all, actions speak louder than words.

Concrete evidence is your key to success. Many people overinflate the things they do in life, but it's hard to argue against what you can prove to be true. You'll want to line up your ducks in a way that is undisputable by supporting your statements with clear and convincing evidence.

To do this, you should employ what I call **The Rule of Four**. The Rule of Four consists of a written journal, relevant pictures, witness testimony, and an email record. These four basic strategies build a foundation of concrete evidence. Each can stand alone, but together they form a solid working armor.

Strategy #1
The Handwritten Journal

The first way to prove the truth of your story is to keep a daily journal. I can't stress the importance of this piece of evidence enough. Though it is just one piece of the puzzle, a journal could be one of the many things the judge might use to decide what custody and visitation plan serves the best interest of your child.

In my opinion, there's an important trick to this. When it comes to journals, a journal kept digitally may not make for the strongest piece of evidence. If you think about it, electronic documents are easy to change and fabricate. However, handwritten pieces are not. That's why I suggest creating an actual paper journal written in pen instead of pencil. It doesn't have to be fancy. A simple notebook will do.

The goal of using this journal is to provide written evidence as to what is happening in your family dynamic, giving the judge an idea of your child's daily routine, who the primary caregiver is, and what would disrupt the balance of this routine. If you have concerns that the other parent is attempting to alienate your child from you, notate specific incidents of parent alienation in your journal. In addition, notate how it is affecting your child. Please be specific. (I discuss parent alienation in more detail starting on page 65.)

In your journal, you will want to give consistent examples of that routine. For example, if you take your child to school or daycare several days a week, the journal can provide factual data to support this. Also, a journal can refresh your memory on important events. It can be a helpful tool when you are putting together your RFO or Responsive Declaration.

Remember that everything counts. A journal can also hurt your case, so you need to be thoughtful as to what you're writing in it. To do this, be honest about the details you provide. Further, don't skip days. If there are entries for two consecutive months, and then a few weeks are missing, the judge may wonder why. Also, the other parent might make the argument that you are cherry picking what you put in your journal.

Keep track of anything that concerns you regarding the other parent's actions, especially when it comes to three things: rebutting accusations that you're not involved in your child's life, disproving statements that you're not the primary caregiver, and shedding light on issues that are going on that you may need to raise at a later date.

Ideally, you want to keep your journal updated and current. In some cases, I know that this may not be possible, but I recommend you make every attempt to achieve this goal. I encourage my clients to keep a daily journal even if there is nothing to report about on a particular day. I also suggest jotting down major events that can shed light on your family dynamics. There may be some legal obstacles in getting your journal into evidence, but journals are proven to be useful tools when used correctly.

Further, remember to keep your journal in a safe place. If you have a safe, use it to lock the journal up so it won't be lost or taken. Also, make two copies of your journal on a regular basis. You can keep the first copy on hand, but the second copy should not be in the house. That said, be careful who you give it to; you don't want the wrong person reading it.

When you're putting entries in your journal, take the time to think about the things that you do for and with your child. Think about what the judge will want to see in the way of patterns. Plus, try to make a large portion of your journal reflect recent events. The past won't carry as much weight to the judge because things change over time.

Here are some examples of questions you may want to answer in your journal:

- Do you prepare meals for your child?
- Do you provide transportation to and from school, daycare, sports, or lessons?
- Do you give your child medications?
- Do you drive to doctor and dentist appointments?
- Do you take your child to social activities like play dates or basketball games?
- What is your child's preference?
- Is your child in therapy? Why is your child in therapy?

You should also include anything that raises a concern regarding the relationship between the child and the other parent. If the other parent rarely sees the child, be sure to note this.

Equally, you should note if you have made an effort to establish a relationship between the child and the other parent. You should also include any incident where the child has been afraid of the other parent or has expressed an unwillingness to have a relationship with the other parent. I can't emphasize this enough: the judge wants to see that you are attempting to co-parent.

STRATEGY #2
THE POWER OF PICTURES

As the old saying goes, a picture is worth a thousand words. That's why pictures can serve as an important piece of evidence in your case. After all, it's hard to dispute what you can physically see.

Begin by gathering existing photos of you with your child. Use these photos as a way to demonstrate past involvement in your child's life and to show how supportive you are as a parent.

Also, make it a habit of taking new pictures on a regular basis, which continues to build on your story. In this process, digitally date your pictures. If the other parent tries to say you're never around, this shows a different side of the equation. Photos that give evidence that you are spending time with your child can go a long way.

New photos can also show many things regarding your child's life. You might show a gathering of extended family that demonstrates your child's connection to the community and how uprooting the child may not serve his or her best interest. You can even show a simple study session, demonstrating that you are a capable parent.

Remember that pictures also have the ability to damage your case, especially as they relate to social media. Evidence is a two-way street. Consequently, posts on social media can make or break you. After all, you never know who's watching your seemingly simple Facebook posts. In general, remember not to give the other parent anything to use against you, whether it be in the form of an emotionally charged text message, email, or social media posting.

There's a useful phrase I teach clients in this respect: "Keep your nose clean." I like clients to refrain from the use of Facebook, Twitter, and Instagram during a custody battle. However, I know that many people feel out of touch with contacts if they do this.

If you are going to continue using these sites, the best way to keep your nose clean is to be careful which pictures and words you post. Think about what the pictures and words you choose say about the quality of your parenting. If you want the judge to adopt your parenting plan, you have to be wise.

Also, make it a habit of deconstructing the messages a picture sends. For example, if the other parent thinks you drink too much, you don't want to post pictures at a sporting event with alcohol in your hand. Sure, you might be having just one beer; however, a judge has no way to know this. This picture could make it look like you have a problem, especially if the other party has said that you do.

The past can also haunt you in this respect. Maybe you partied a lot seven years ago and had a lot to drink when you partied. You were not home often with your child, but you've changed. You are older and more mature now. However, it would not be wise to post pictures of you partying with a beer in your hand even if it is at your best friend's bachelor's party. Sure, you can most likely explain it away should the other parent attempt to use it against you, but do you want the headache of having to do so? An angry parent may try to use the pictures to argue that you are still drinking and partying.

It's also important to think about what a picture says about your values. For example, raunchy photos may paint a picture that can contribute to a smear campaign. You just never know what the other parent may present out of context or how someone might perceive it.

To avoid common mishaps relating to photos, think of some scenarios of pictures that won't serve you well. Further, consider tightening up your profile's settings so that you limit what others see and have to approve pictures others tag you in before they appear on your timeline.

Also, know that the power of pictures can transcend far beyond your own behaviors. You can also use pictures to show patterns related to the other parent. For example, if the other parent passes out on the couch and you're trying to prove that he has a drinking problem, a picture can add weight to this.

At the end of the day, your goal is to prove to the judge why he should approve your proposed parenting plan. This mentality goes back to the court's standard of acting in the best interest of the child. Pictures can be a powerful tool to give the judge insight, but if taken lightly, they can harm your case. As a practical tip, do not speak ill of the other parent on social media and do not encourage others to do so. Words can come back to haunt you; they can be used against you in court and may not go over well with the judge.

Strategy #3
The Witness Testimony

Next, you will want to put together a list of people who will attest to the facts you've stated in your case. These witnesses will help prove that what you've said is true.

As previously noted, a judge will be looking for what serves the best interest of the child while considering many factors. Witnesses can separate the truth from fiction.

In the process of choosing witnesses, a common mistake that many people make in court is relying solely on family members and close friends for testimonials. These people do have important things to say, and I encourage you to include their statements in your RFO or Responsive Declaration if it will shed light on important issues. However, a judge will expect friends and family to say good things about you, whereas a testimony from a neutral third party most likely will hold more weight. You want the strongest possible lineup if you need witnesses to testify on your behalf.

So where do you begin when choosing neutral third-party witnesses?

There are three places to look: school, extracurricular activities, and the community in which you live or grew up. In the school department, for example, teachers are great resources. They are always around, seeing your relationship and involvement with your child. They're also examples of individuals who have no reason not to tell the truth. Similarly, coaches can give accounts of excellent parenting in the way of extracurricular activities.

Respected community leaders can be good witnesses too, giving weight to your case.

Unfortunately, it can be difficult to get these people on board. For example, teachers don't usually like to get involved in custody battles. That said, there is a way around this. You can **subpoena** a teacher if he or she is not willing to give testimony. A subpoena is a court order issued at the request of a party in a lawsuit that requires an individual who is not a party in the lawsuit to do something such as appearing in court.

At the end of the day, remember to keep a good relationship with all of the authority figures in your child's life. Sure, a coach or teacher might anger you by seeming to favor the other parent, but rocking the boat will not serve you well. This person may testify on the other parent's behalf, which could ultimately hurt your case. Please be careful what you say in front of a possible witness. Your words might come back to bite you.

STRATEGY #4
THE EMAIL RECORD

Finally, emails can be an excellent strategy to build evidence. You can employ this resource by using emails to communicate when conflicts with the other parent arise, giving you a traceable record. For example, if the other parent drops the ball on an arranged visitation, an email record of your communication can help to prove this. Also, emails can show that you're easy to work with.

An example of an email for a missed visitation might look like this:

Dear John,

It's 2 p.m. on Saturday. You were supposed to be here at 1 p.m., but you haven't arrived yet. We talked about this. You agreed not to be late to arranged visitations, but it's still going on. What can we do to work this out?

- Jane

It's also important to note that emails can hurt your case. If your emails appear overbearing, petty, or harassing in nature—this can hurt you. To avoid harming your case, be careful what you write. Make sure your child is the center of the email. In other words, this is not a time to argue with the other parent for cheating on you in the past.

Although you probably have strong emotions when it comes to the other parent, judges do not want to read about your past love life. In fact, the other parent can use emotionally charged emails against you. A seasoned attorney may use emails like these to prove that you are emotionally unstable. This is a way to try to gain leverage in a custody battle.

As a side note, do not make any verbal or written threats to the other parent. You may end up with a restraining order against you. If you do, this can negatively affect your custody case. In fact, there is a possibility that you will be ordered supervised visitations for a lengthy period of time if the restraining order is granted.

I know custody and visitation cases can be emotionally taxing, and people may say things that they do not mean out of pain and anger. However, this is a sure way to lose the battle before you even get started.

Of course, there are those times when a restraining order is necessary. If you need protection for yourself and your children because the other parent has threatened your safety, I strongly urge you to seek a restraining order requesting supervised visitations to the other parent. You should not live in fear, and a restraining order is one way to protect you and your children. The judge will ultimately make the final decision on whether there is good cause to grant a permanent restraining order.

Some courts offer free assistance to victims of domestic violence by helping individuals fill out forms necessary to request a restraining order. These services may provide support by having a third party show up to the court with you. You can also request a third party to sit at the table with you during your hearing in court if you are a victim of domestic violence.

CHAPTER 3

THE INS AND OUTS OF MEDIATION

No one knows your child like you do. Plain and simple.

Judges do their best to protect children, but at the end of the day, they don't really know your child. They don't know the specks of color in your child's eyes or the exact color of your child's hair. They don't know your child's favorite ice cream. They don't know what songs your child likes. Most importantly, they don't know what your child dislikes.

All they know about your child is from the evidence they get from you, the other parent, and from third parties.

To protect the best interest of your child, you need to know what options the judge may give you in the way of settling custody issues. One of these options is something called **mediation**.

Please note that the official name for the concept of mediation depends on the county in which you live. For example, in Riverside and San Bernardino, courts call mediation "Child Custody Recommending Counseling" or CCRC.

So, what is mediation?

Mediation is a means by which a trained third party helps parents develop a parenting plan. It is court-ordered, and the mediator works in the courthouse where the judge will hear your case. The purpose of the mediation process is to get the parties to come to an agreement. The upside of mediation, in general, is that it is one way to end the battle. It is extremely helpful when both parties can join together to come up with a parenting plan that both parents believe is in the best interest of their child.

The Difference Between a Non-Reporting County and a Reporting County

Family courts in California are required to have a mediation department. Different counties may have different names for their mediation department but the goal is the same – to get the parents to agree on a parenting plan. Each county is either a Reporting County or Non-Reporting County. Please check your local court rules to determine if your county is a Non-Reporting or Reporting county.

The first thing you need to know about mediation is the difference between a Non-Reporting County and a Reporting County, and whether or not you live in a Reporting County. This information is important if you are in a custody and visitation battle with the other parent.

In a **Non-Reporting County** such as Los Angeles County or Orange County, the mediation is a confidential process, which means the mediator will NOT make a custody and visitation recommendation to the judge. If you and the other parent are unable to agree on a parenting plan, the mediator will send a notice to the judge that you and the other parent were not able to come to an agreement. You and the other parent will have an opportunity to argue your case in front of the judge. The judge will make temporary custody and visitation orders at the hearing after hearing oral arguments for both parents.

The judge can also order the parents to participate in a child custody evaluation to gain more insight into the family dynamics. The judge will most likely set another date for you and the other parent to return. In the interim, the judge will probably make temporary orders.

Please note that if the judge orders you to participate in a custody evaluation, that evaluator will render a written report to the judge with his custody and visitation recommendations. The evaluator may even be called to testify about his report and recommendations.

In **Reporting Counties** such as Riverside and San Bernardino, mediators provide the judge with a written report that contains temporary custody and visitation recommendations. You will have an opportunity to review the mediator's recommendation (usually the morning of the hearing). Mediators base their recommendations upon what takes place in the mediation sessions, reports from third-party experts, the parents' declarations, and the evidence filed in court along with other relevant factors.

Judges in these counties often rely on a mediator's recommendation to make temporary child custody and visitation orders, meaning recommendations in Reporting Counties carry a lot of weight.

I often tell my clients that in Reporting Counties, mediation can make or break your custody case. I cannot stress enough how important it is to prepare for mediation. Attorneys do not participate in mediation, so it will be up to you to convince the mediator why your proposed parenting plan is in the best interest of your child. Remember, mediation isn't just a chance to convince the mediator that your plan is the best plan; it is an opportunity for you and the other parent to agree on a parenting plan.

If you agree on a parenting plan, the mediator will not make a recommendation to the judge.

In a Reporting County, the judge is still the person who will make the ultimate custody and visitation decision. He will decide whether to adopt the recommendation in its entirety, adopt only parts of the recommendation, or adopt none of the recommendation. Again, because judges rely on mediators for guidance, judges will give the recommendation a lot of weight.

If you do not agree with the recommendation, it can be an uphill battle to convince a judge that he should not adopt the mediation recommendation on at least a temporary basis.

Tips for a Successful Mediation Session

Mediators have the power of 10 in the eyes of the judge. Consequently, treat mediation with the same respect as an official court date. Try to be polite and cooperative. Understand that in general, mediators and judges look for an interest in fostering a good relationship with the other parent. The goal of the mediator is to get both parents to settle the case. If the mediator believes you are an uncooperative parent, that could strongly affect the end result of your case.

It's equally important to be timely when it comes to documentation that mediators receive. If you're the respondent, file your Responsive Declaration at least five business days before mediation regardless of your court date. This is important because your Responsive Declaration is your opportunity to tell your side of the story and explain why your proposed parenting plan is in the best interest of your child before the mediation starts.

In addition to being polite and cooperative, you must also be firm. If you believe that a parenting plan is not in the best interest of your child, you shouldn't cave in only to make the other parent happy. Your child's wellbeing is what is most important.

When it comes to mediation, there are some ways you can show the mediator that you put the best interest of your child first and want to be cooperative in reaching a parenting plan with the other parent. First, don't use the phrase "my child" during mediation because it may seem as though you don't want to share. Instead, make it a point to say, "our child." You'll come across as more of a team player.

Another tool as means of leading the effort to work together is to suggest that both parents attend co-parenting classes. If the other parent suggests this option first, be wary of disagreeing. If you say, "Absolutely not," but don't give a good reason as to why you disagree with a co-parenting class, it could look like you're not making an effort to work together. The mediator might include this in her report, which may not go over well.

There are also general standards that you should be aware of when it comes to the mediation process. Mediation usually only involves the parents. In other words, mediators will not allow a new love interest or spouse to participate. If the other parent has abused you in the past, you can request a separate interview. The abusive parent will be able to participate in the mediation but will do so in a separate mediation session.

The mediator may also interview age-appropriate children as a general part of this process, which involves a separate meeting from the meeting with the parents. In general, interviews with children are important because a child's interview can give the mediator and judge more insight as to what is going on in the family dynamics.

A child's interview can also shed light on what the child's preferences are as to where he or she wants to live. Also, interviews can reveal certain issues regarding each parent. For example, if one parent claims the other parent is an alcoholic and the other parent denies it, a child's interview can help confirm or deny this accusation. Please note that a child's preference becomes more relevant when the child is 14 years of age or older.

When it comes to interviews with children, the mediator may be looking for signs of coaching. Unfortunately, some parents coach their children before mediation, which can be stressful for the child and create unnecessary anxiety. If you suspect coaching, you should bring this up immediately in your declaration to the judge as well as in mediation. You may also want to request a mediation appointment on a day when your child will be with you. In doing so, you can bring your child to the mediation appointment to keep the other parent from coaching the child right before mediation.

Remember that mediation is an opportunity for you and the other parent to come up with a parenting plan agreement for your child. When it comes to mediation, ask yourself the following: Would you rather work out a plan with the other parent or let the judge—who may have the best of intentions but doesn't really know your child—decide what the arrangement will be? Also, please remember that the mediator can include in her report any and all communications that occurred in mediation in reporting counties. Therefore, you want to be careful what you say as your words may end up in court.

What If You Do Not Agree with the Recommendation?

Fortunately, if you do not agree with the mediator's recommendation, you have options.

First, you will have an opportunity at your hearing to review the recommendation and make oral arguments in court as to why you disagree with it. As a practical tip, you should ask the mediator if you can pick up her recommendation days before the hearing. You'll want as much time as possible to review the recommendation and prepare for court. If you do not agree with the recommendation in its entirety or in part, you'll want to be prepared to tell the judge why.

If you agree with the recommendation, your job will be easier but don't rest on your laurels. As the other parent may be able to make a convincing argument as to why the judge should not adopt the mediation report, you'll need to be prepared to argue why the judge should. Because you will have a solid RFO or Responsive Declaration filed, you can direct the judge to your declaration and to the attached evidence to help you with your argument.

Secondly, you can request another mediation with a different mediator. You can make this request orally at your custody and visitation hearing. However, it is discretionary, and the judge will ultimately decide if your case should be re-referred to mediation. If a judge does

NOT grant your request for a different mediator but grants your request for a new mediation, you can request a different mediator at the mediation office (depending on the county). In some counties, you will have to go through a process with the mediation department in requesting a new mediator. As mentioned earlier, it is important to understand the mediation process in your county to know how to navigate through the system.

You also have the option to request a Child Custody 730 Evaluation. A 730 Evaluation is a more in-depth analysis of the family dynamics than mediation. It involves a court-appointed mental health professional such as a psychologist interviewing, observing and assessing the family members to give the judge feedback on the family dynamics.

The evaluation is a lengthy process; it can take months before a report with the evaluator's recommendations are complete.

A 730 Evaluation usually consists of the following:

- Interviews with each parent alone to discuss her/her childhood, concerns about the other parent, family dynamics, parenting skills and any other relevant information as it relates to the children.
- Personality and psychological tests for the parents. These tests give the evaluator and the judge insight on you as a person, including whether or not you are a cooperative parent with the other parent.
- Interviews with the child if age appropriate. Often times, the evaluator will interview the child alone and then will observe the child interact with each parent.

- Review of documents such as motions filed with the court, third-party witness statements and any other evidence provided by the parents or the parents' attorneys.
- Telephone or in-person interviews with third parties who can give insight on the parents' characters. This can include therapists, teachers, family members or any other person that has valuable information regarding the family dynamic. As a practical tip, if you would like the evaluator to interview a specific third party, let the evaluator know and provide him the contact information.

The judge will consider the evaluator's recommendation in making final custody and visitation orders. Some judges may appoint a 730 evaluator on its own motion, especially if there is a major custody dispute where the judge needs more information to make a decision. Other times, a 730 evaluator can be appointed by one party making an oral request at a custody and visitation hearing. In rare cases, you will need to file a motion requesting the court appoint a 730 evaluator in your case.

In some jurisdictions, the court has a list of approved 730 evaluators and would prefer that the parties choose an evaluator from the approved list. The judge will either select an evaluator or order the parents to select one. You will want to choose an evaluator carefully. For example, if you have a concern that the other parent is alienating you from your child, you will want to be sure that the evaluator you choose has experience dealing with the issue of parent alienation. If you have hired an attorney, ask the attorney which 730 evaluator might be best suited to your case and why.

The benefit of a 730 Evaluation is that it is a more in-depth look into the family dynamic than mediation. It carries a lot of weight with the court and will most likely supersede an undesirable recommendation from a mediator. Similar to mediation, a 730 Evaluation can make or break your case. I cannot stress enough how important it is to prepare for your 730 Evaluation and to make sure all the evidence that you would like to present to the evaluator has been filed with the court and served on the other party.

The main disadvantage of a 730 Evaluation is the hefty price tag. Depending on the county, the costs can start at $4,000. If there is a significant disparity in income, you may want to request that the other parent pay for the evaluation. Unless you and the other parent can agree on how to pay for the evaluation, the judge will decide who pays. The evaluator will not start working on the case until either you or the other parent has paid the costs in full.

Another disadvantage is that the process of a 730 Evaluation takes place outside of court. Therefore, it may take several months before the judge receives the report. In the meantime, the judge's temporary orders will remain in full force (unless there is good cause to modify the orders before the judge receives the report).

If the evaluator recommends a parenting plan that you do not want, it can be a challenge to convince a judge to not adopt the recommendation. It is even a steeper hill to climb if both the mediator's recommendation and the 730 Evaluation are not in your favor.

However, it's important to remember that the judge makes the final decision. If you truly believe that the evaluator got it wrong, you may consider filing a motion with the court requesting a 733 Evaluation. In essence, you can request a new evaluation with a different evaluator. The judge will most likely make you pay for the 733 Evaluation if he grants your request.

Similar to mediation, you will have an opportunity at a later date to challenge the 730 Evaluation at trial.

The following are examples of why a parent might request a new mediator or a 730 Evaluation:

- The parent feels his or her concerns were not addressed during mediation.
- There was a language barrier that made it difficult for that parent to communicate.
- The mediator did not read the file or reference in his report concerns that should have been evident by reading the Responsive Declaration, RFO, and third-party declarations.
- The parent believes the mediator was biased and made statements during mediation that raised a concern regarding her neutrality.
- The parent believes the other parent has a mental issue that has gone undetected.
- If there is evidence of parent alienation and child coaching, but the mediator did not address those issues.
- If circumstances have changed to warrant a more in-depth look into the family dynamics.

CHAPTER 4

THE DANGERS OF PARENT ALIENATION AND HOW TO COMBAT IT

Children may simply feel naturally closer to one parent than the other. However, another reason for this type of dynamic is a well-researched concept called parental alienation.

How many older children or young adults have told you that they were close to just one parent after a divorce?

Many factors contribute to this sort of family dynamic.

Parent alienation is when one parent attempts to alienate the child from the other parent. In short, parental alienation happens when a child is subject to negative comments and circumstances revolving around the other parent. Studies have documented this concept. The intent of parent alienation is to destroy the bond between the child and the other parent.

Parents may engage in parental alienation in a number of ways, sometimes without thinking about it. First, one parent may speak badly about the other parent, feeding the child with negative messages that program negative thoughts.

Another example of parental alienation is when one parent tries to prevent the child from seeing the other parent. For example, one parent may book numerous activities designed to keep a child busy, preventing the other parent from visiting with the child.

In addition, some parents try to manipulate how much a child talks to the other parent. They might take the child's phone away or punish the child for speaking to the other parent. Some parents even find reasons for a child to have to get off the phone with the other parent during conversations.

Parents may also try to confuse a child by sending mixed messages. For example, a parent may tell a child that the other parent doesn't love him. A parent may also have a child refer to a stepparent or love interest as Mom or Dad.

These are very real methods of parental alienation. If you do suspect parental alienation, there are many things you can do, but you must take action immediately. The longer parental alienation goes on, the more it will confuse the child and destroy your relationship with the child. In addition, it can leave the child with long-lasting emotional scars.

So how should you deal with parental alienation if you suspect that the other parent has exposed your child to these types of tactics?

First, make it a point to create open channels of communication with your child to combat any false impressions your child might have. That said, remember not to discuss your court case with your child or speak negatively about the other parent.

Second, make sure you document what is happening. Write this in your journal with the time and date you became aware of it. Also, send a short, informal email to the other parent and use it as evidence later. Your intent should be to communicate and document the situation.

You can say something like this:

John,

It has come to my attention that you told Jimmy that I don't love him. He has expressed voluntarily that you have told him this on more than one occasion. I'm not sure if this is true, but if it is, I ask that it stop immediately. Our first interest is to protect Jimmy. We need to show him that we both love him.

- Jane

This communication demonstrates to the judge that you're putting the child first and that in trying to address this, you're being amicable. Judges can't stand bickering. They want parents to try to work it out, and this type of communication shows that you're making a reasonable effort.

If this doesn't end parental alienation, the next step is to file an RFO. You want to document the parental alienation. In your RFO, you may want to request that the judge appoint an expert to dig deeper into the parental alienation, especially if the judge is not convinced that there is parental alienation.

As discussed previously, the judge may appoint a 730 evaluator to address this issue.

Point out specific incidents supported by third-party witnesses, emails, and any other evidence that will support your claims of parental alienation. In addition, highlight how the other parent's actions are affecting your child, particularly if your child appears depressed, makes random, untrue statements about you, or more frequently displays moods such as anger and sadness. Be specific with your examples.

As a practical tip, make sure to keep the focus on your child more so than your feelings towards your ex. Your feelings may be justified, but it is important to focus on your child's happiness and making sure you convey your concerns in an emotionally stable manner.

Please note that if the judge finds that one parent is alienating the other parent, the judge could order the child to live primarily with the parent who is not alienating. Also, if you believe that your child is suffering emotionally due to the alienation, you may want to consider requesting therapy for the child.

Always remember that regardless of the age of the child, a divorce or custody proceeding will directly impact him. Children recognize far more than we credit them for. I can't stress enough how important it is to foster a healthy relationship between the child and each parent to reduce the emotional impact a custody battle will have on the children.

CHAPTER 5

HOW TO SHINE IN COURT

Shining in court takes everything from preparation to respect. It's a unified effort designed to present your case in the best possible light.

Shining in court is a process that begins quietly. That's why your first step should be to go to court as an observer. To do this, take the time to watch and listen by sitting in on your judge's proceedings before your court date arrives. Observing will teach you a lot.

It's important not to sidestep this effort by thinking that observing any judge will do. Every judge is different. Some may favor one action, while others may not. Therefore, you want to watch the actual judge assigned to your case.

There are times when the courtroom may be full, and the deputies only allow people who have cases on the calendar that day to sit in and listen. In this case, I encourage you to speak to an attorney who works in that courtroom often. The attorney may be able to give insight on what is important and not important to that judge as it relates to your case.

It's important to remember that different judges take different stances. You never know which stance your judge will take regarding your actions, so it's best to err on the side of caution. A good example of this can be the drinking behaviors mentioned earlier. It's okay to have a social drink here and there, but think about it in the sense of how a judge will view your life. You don't want a child to say, "Yes, I see Mommy [or Daddy] drinking a lot." It's all about the picture you paint. You're telling a story, and the judge is going to form opinions based on the information he does or doesn't have.

Also, it's good to know the rules of your county and the rules of the court where your hearing will take place.

There are different rules in different counties, so your goal should be to familiarize yourself with the local rules.

For instance, if you seek an emergency hearing in Riverside, you must file the day before, so if you file paperwork on Monday, the hearing will take place on Tuesday. However, in Los Angeles, emergency hearings can take place on the same day the paperwork is filed.

A good way to become familiar with the rules of your county is by talking to a Family Law attorney who regularly litigates in that county. You can also use local court websites as a resource. These websites will give you access to forms and the county local rules.

When it comes to the legal system, it's important to remember that your life is in the spotlight. Courts may look at legal records and obtain written reports from outside parties. For example, they may receive psychologist reports, police reports, reports from teachers, and reports from therapists. Think about exactly what the judge may receive as you go about planning your case.

How to Dress in Court

Let's face it—first impressions are important. People dress in all sorts of ways in court, but this isn't always a good thing.

When it comes to how to dress, I tell my clients to skip the overly casual and dress nicely. You want to dress like you're going to church or a business meeting. Your goal is to look clean-cut. After all, you are representing your children.

Also, it's important to dress nicely because some judges won't let you into a courtroom if your clothing is inappropriate. You want to convey respect to the judge and his courtroom through the way you dress.

When it comes to dress, there are some definite "do nots" on my list. First of all, do not wear shorts or flip-flops. Also, do not wear baseball caps as many judges consider caps disrespectful. Jeans are okay if they're nice jeans, but this wouldn't be my first suggestion (especially if they're too baggy or too tight). And ladies, keep the cleavage out of court. Seriously. Even the nicest of tops can come off as showing a little too much. Finally, be wary of showing tattoos. When in doubt, cover them up.

So, what should you wear in court?

To determine appropriate attire, pretend you're meeting with a community leader or going to church. What would you wear? You wouldn't dress in formalwear, but you wouldn't dress as if you are going to a sporting event either. Your goal would be to dress conservatively. You would err cautiously and play it safe. Do the same when you're going to court.

How to Find the Right Attorney

Finding the right attorney can be challenging. Although not required, many litigants in custody battles hire an attorney to represent them and the interests of their children. I suggest that you start looking for an attorney before you need one. Look for one that has family law experience. You can do this by looking at referral services, asking a friend, searching Google or other search engines, or visiting the courthouse where your case may be heard to observe the different attorneys.

I recommend narrowing your attorney search down to three attorneys and then setting up in-person interviews with all three. You will want to inquire about their experience, how often they appear in that particular courthouse, and how long they have been practicing family law. You also want to do independent research to determine their reputation in the community. For example, is she someone who seems to care about her cases or does she have a cavalier attitude about her cases? Does he appear to be ethical? You need to know what you are looking for in an attorney. You may want to inquire as to what the office's policy is for keeping clients informed of the progress of the case as well as the attorney's caseload. You want to ensure that the attorney has the time to dedicate to your case. It is important that you feel comfortable with the attorney you choose.

Please note that attorneys can be quite expensive. Most family law attorneys charge per hour. Attorneys' rates vary, but the typical range for a seasoned family law attorney is $300 to $600 per hour.

How to Argue Your Case

Arguing a case in court on your own takes skill and planning. It's not easy to do, but it is possible. That's what you're going to learn in this section.

I've watched many cases of people who represent themselves in court. In my experience, there is a consistent pattern in the way of success. People who succeed speak concisely and articulate their thoughts well. These two factors seem to make judges listen, so you need to get to the point.

In fact, I can't stress the importance of being concise enough. Nine times out of ten, you don't have a long period of time to speak; it's crucial to make your words count. Also, try to stay away from using slang. The judge may or may not understand it. In the end, it is important that you be yourself, be confident and know that you are there for your child.

It's also important to be clear in what you're trying to say. To do this, create an ultimate result (also known as a conclusion) backed by three to five reasons why the judge should adopt your parenting plan. For example, your result may be that you should have primary custody because your child has lived with you for the last five years. You'll want to provide reasons as to why the child living with you is in his best interest. You'll want to discuss any emotional impact a change in the living arrangements will have on your child.

When it comes to this process, this is your opportunity to point out evidence that you already provided to the judge that can support your argument. If your child confirmed what you're saying with the mediator and it is in the mediator's report, you should reference that report. Also, if you have school records that show that the child attends school in the district where you reside, turn the judge's attention to the record. Just remember to practice what you're going to say before you go to court instead of speaking in an improvisational manner.

Another way to argue the case is to find inconsistencies in the other parent's story and cast doubt on the other parent's credibility. Do not be afraid to use the mediator's report if it substantiates the issues you've raised in your RFO or Responsive Declaration. If the mediator confirms that the other parent has only seen your child a handful of times that year, and the other parent boasts that he sees the child on a regular basis, this is your opportunity to point out these inconsistencies.

Also, make an attempt to follow the judge's direction. For example, if the judge has a concern that he needs you to address, it would be prudent for you to address this concern. In preparing for court, expect the unexpected. You can prepare all day long, but the judge may have specific questions he wants you to answer.

Further, remember to start with what's most important first because you might not get through everything you want to say. Judges can cut you off, especially if you're rambling. This is why watching your judge beforehand is important. You'll know the judge's style. You'll also know his temperament and an average of how long the judge gives people to speak.

That said, when it comes to being concise, don't speak to the judge in general terms. The judge won't know if what you're describing happened ten years or one day ago; it's okay to give approximate dates. You might say, "Since January of 2010, our children have been living with me primarily," or, "Within the last six months, Mr. John has seen our child ten times." Give the judge statements backed up by facts.

This is where the initial declaration that you wrote in an RFO or a Responsive Declaration becomes important. You want to make sure what you wrote is detailed so that you can reference these declarations. In general, it also helps to assume that the judge hasn't read your documents and doesn't know your case as well as you do. Use this time to educate the judge on your case and why it is in the best interest of your child for the judge to adopt your proposed parenting plan.

Also, feel free to reference third-party testimonials as a means of backing up your story. You can say something like, "I would like to turn the judge's attention to the declaration of Mary Johnson, who stated that…" At this point, you would fill in the blanks as to what Mary Johnson said and why it is relevant.

Know what arguments the other parent will make and be ready to address them. Think outside the box. You know the other parent better than the judge does and probably can predict how he will conduct himself in court. Have an answer already in mind for any point that he may make. If the other parent makes a false statement, be prepared to tell the court that it is not true and why it is not true.

Lastly, be courteous but firm. Please do not talk over the judge or the other parent, but do not be afraid to speak up. If there is a point that you believe is crucial to your case, let the judge know that and ask that he give you a brief moment to explain.

At this time, the court should make temporary custody and visitation orders.

If you are happy with the judge's temporary orders, you may want to request the judge to set a trial date to determine final custody and visitation orders. As discussed earlier, unless something changes, judges are reluctant to grossly change a temporary order that is working for the children.

What if the Judge Doesn't Agree with Your Request?

As previously stated, family law is an art, not a science. The human element plays its part, and we often find that family law is a world of subjectivity. You can argue your case at the hearing, hitting on all the relevant points, and the judge still may not see it the same way you do. You may be left feeling helpless and confused, but there are still things you can do to try to rehabilitate your case.

First, you can request the court set a review hearing on the issue of custody and visitation in a couple of months. This is a great strategy if you believe that the court is not ready to adopt your parenting plan at that moment but may be willing to step up to it if you satisfy specific court orders such as attending a parenting class or exercising your visitations on a consistent basis.

A review hearing will give you another opportunity to argue your case and to show the judge what steps you have taken to address his concerns. As a practical tip, you will want to file a supplemental declaration with the court before your review hearing, outlining what things you have done to address the judge's concerns. Also, you will want to make sure to serve the other party with your supplemental declaration along with any accompanying evidence.

Secondly, you may want to request a hearing with live witness testimony if you think the court may be swayed by hearing from your witnesses in person. Live witness testimony may help your case by shedding light on certain issues. Be careful, as live witnesses can also destroy your case, especially if their testimonies are different from their written statements.

You will need to know whether your court allows live testimony on the day of the hearing or whether you need to request a future date from the judge. Once again, this will depend on the judge, but you can call the courtroom to get a better understanding of that court's policies and procedures. Always remember to be polite to the clerk and other court staff members as the judge could easily learn of any rude behavior. For further information, review California Family Code Section 217.

Next, you can request the judge to order a 730 Evaluation, as previously discussed, if you need an expert to take a more in-depth look into the family dynamics. It should be noted that a 730 Evaluation is typically ordered to gear up for trial. The judge will most likely make final custody and visitation orders at trial.

Further, you can file another RFO requesting a modification of the currents orders. As a practical tip, do not file an RFO right after your hearing (unless there is a material change in circumstances or a valid emergency). Instead, wait until some time has passed. In this new RFO, you will need to show why a modification of the judge's orders will be in the best interest of your child. It would be prudent to explain what has changed since the last time you were in court. Remember to include third-party witness statements and evidence to support your RFO.

Lastly, you can always try to speak to the other parent about coming to an agreement. I encourage co-parenting, and this is ultimately the best way to end the battle before you have to go to war.

If you need helping filling out forms, please visit your local courthouse to determine if there is a free service to assist you. Also, you can call your county's local bar association. Some bar associations have clinics that will help you with document preparation. Another way to begin document preparation is to visit your county's court website to download forms.

In closing, always remember that child custody and visitation orders are modifiable. Stay confident and know that you are further ahead today than you were yesterday. And remember, children are resilient. With your continued support and love, your child will weather this storm as well.

EPILOGUE

Now that you've reached the end of this book, I encourage you to ponder all that you've learned. You now have some knowledge of the child custody and visitation process. You also know the importance of record keeping and how to correctly keep those records. Also, you know which forms to file and how to respond. You even know how to compile compelling evidence and the appropriate way to argue your case in court.

Remember that a child custody and visitation case is a process. It takes careful planning and time. It is not easy and sometimes even not fair. Trust me—I completely understand! At the end of the day, please remember that your child is the most important person in this process.

This book only covers California family law. The laws are constantly changing. If you're still struggling, be sure to talk to an experienced attorney who can help you in this time of need and guide you in ways that you might not have thought of.

Take care and keep your chin up!

Shauna M. Albright

ACKNOWLEDGEMENTS

Thank you to my friends, family members, colleagues, and those I have met along the way who have, in some way or another, been an inspiration to me in writing this book.

A heartfelt thank you to my husband and my loving daughter for showing me unconditional love. I love you with all my heart and could not have written this book without your support!

AUTHOR BIOGRAPHY

Shauna M. Albright is the Founder and Managing Attorney at the Law Offices of Shauna M. Albright, located in Riverside, California. As one of the few firms that handle family law cases exclusively, her office has helped countless people successfully move on from the often-painful and complicated process of divorce and child custody.

Recognized for her legal excellence by her peers, Ms. Albright has received awards and commendations from various California state representatives. She has been featured in the *San Bernardino Sun* as "Someone to Know" and has served as a board member for various nonprofits dedicated to helping individuals with family law matters. Ms. Albright is a staunch advocate for educating our youth and has served as the Chair of the Education committee for the Richard. T. Fields Bar Association.

In addition to being an attorney, Ms. Albright was a television news reporter and segment producer for *Evening Edition* on KVCR Channel 24, a PBS member station. She also co-hosted local San Bernardino talk show *Inland Empire Alive*.

In 2019, Ms. Albright was elected as President of the Richard T. Fields Bar Association Foundation, a non-profit organization dedicated to raising scholarship monies for individuals attending college and law school.

For more information about Ms. Albright or to contact her about speaking at an event, visit www.albrightfamilylaw.com or www.shaunaalbright.com.